I KNOW
PEOPLE
AROUND TOWN

By Colin Matthews

Gareth Stevens
PUBLISHING

first concepts

I know people around my town.

This is a
police officer.

5

This is a firefighter.

This is a doctor.

This is a teacher.

This is a mail carrier.

13

This is a dentist.

14

This is a chef.

This is a veterinarian.

18

This is a librarian.

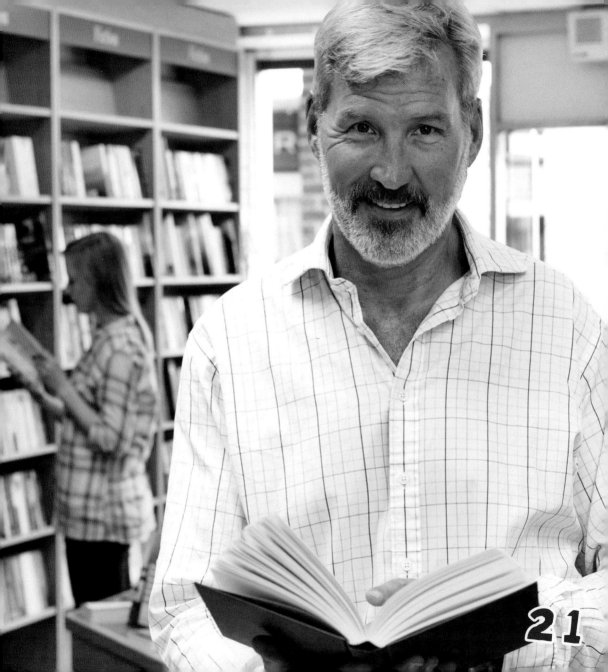

21

Which people around town do you know?

23

Please visit our website, www.garethstevens.com. For a free color catalog of all our high-quality books, call toll free 1-800-542-2595 or fax 1-877-542-2596.

Cataloging-in-Publication Data

Names: Matthews, Colin.
Title: I know people around town / Colin Matthews.
Description: New York : Gareth Stevens Publishing, 2018. | Series: What I know
Identifiers: ISBN 9781482463019 (pbk.) | ISBN 9781482463033 (library bound) | ISBN 9781482463026 (6 pack)
Subjects: LCSH: Municipal services–Juvenile literature. | Professions–Juvenile literature. | Cities and towns–Juvenile literature.
Classification: LCC HD4431.M38 2018 | DDC 331.7–dc23

First Edition

Published in 2018 by
Gareth Stevens Publishing
111 East 14th Street, Suite 349
New York, NY 10003

Designer: Sarah Liddell
Editor: Therese Shea

Photo credits: Cover, p. 1 (stripes) Eky Studio/Shutterstock.com; cover, pp. 1 (dentist), 15 michaeljung/Shutterstock.com; cover, pp. 1 (librarian), 21 SpeedKingz/Shutterstock.com; cover, pp. 1 (firefighter), 7 Tyler Olson/Shutterstock.com; cover, pp. 1 (teacher), 11 Monkey Business Images/Shutterstock.com; p. 3 mTaira/Shutterstock.com; p. 5 pio3/Shutterstock.com; p. 9 Blend Images/Shutterstock.com; p. 13 Joseph Sohm/Shutterstock.com; p. 17 wavebreakmedia/Shutterstock.com; p. 19 Andresr/Shutterstock.com; p. 23 Rawpixel.com/Shutterstock.com.

Printed in the United States of America

CPSIA compliance information: Batch #CS17GS: For further information contact Gareth Stevens, New York, New York at 1-800-542-2595.